Billy is a boy who lives next to the forest.

Every day Billy pretends that he is a great explorer; examining things up close and studying things from far away.

The different colors of leaves, the many shape of rocks, and of course all the animals in the forest fascinated him.

Billy's favorite place to study in the forest is down the hill by a small river. He knows animals get thirsty and will go to the small river to drink the cold water.

One morning Billy awoke with determination; He wanted to go searching for something only a couple of people had seen before: The white fox.

Billy got out of bed, put on his lucky explorer hat, packed his studying tools, and went to the forest, walking down the hill toward the small river.

While Billy sat, waiting patiently, he noticed something or someone scooping up the water with its hands to drink.

Being in the forest, Billy was so excited to meet someone who was just as passionate about exploring as he was. Billy quickly packed up his exploring tools and began walking quickly in order to say hello.

"Hi, my name's Billy! Are you exploring too?"
Billy asked.

"No," Bigfoot replied. "I'm just thirsty because I have been walking all day and needed some water. What are you looking for?"

"Well, there's a white fox in these woods, so I'm trying to see it." Billy said.

Billy liked Bigfoot right away.
Bigfoot had really big feet and really big hands.

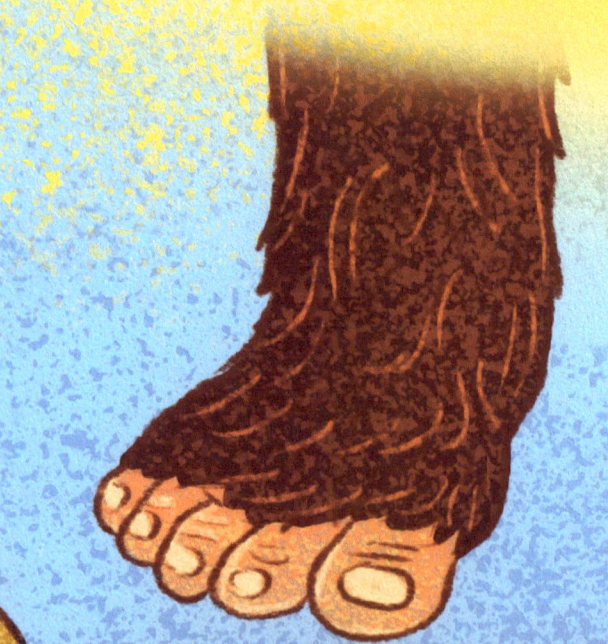

Want to see my studying spot?" Billy asked.
"Ok," said Bigfoot.
Bigfoot was not a creature of many words.

Walking back up the path, Billy showed Bigfoot his favorite spot in the whole forest and pointed to all the different colors of the leaves, the many shapes of the rocks and some of the animals that crossed their path or flew above them, high in the sky.

"This is where I like to study, but sometimes, I don't see anything." Billy explained.

Bigfoot was beginning to really like Billy too.

Bigfoot liked Billy's appreciation for all the different colored leaves, the many shapes of the rocks,

and the animals that lived within the forest or flew above, high in the sky.

"Billy, I think there's a better studying spot on top of that boulder," Bigfoot exclaimed, pointing to a really big rock.

Billy and Bigfoot walked over to the big boulder. With his really big hands and really big feet,

Bigfoot helped Billy climb up on top. As Billy stood on top of the boulder, he could not believe his eyes.

Not only could Billy see down the river, but Billy also could see even more colors of leaves, the animals in the forest and birds flying high in the sky.

Bigfoot looked at Billy and smiled.
"The forest is beautiful, Billy. Now that you can see everything, I must be going," said Bigfoot.

"Will I ever see you again?"
Billy asked.
Bigfoot just smiled, patted
Billy's head and began to walk
away. Billy smiled as he watched
Bigfoot disappear into
the forest.

As it was beginning to get dark, Billy headed back home. Billy was a little sad for not having seen the very rare white fox, but still was happy that he had found a new studying spot on top of the big boulder.

Later that evening, as Billy's parents were tucking him into bed, they told him the story of an unknown animal that lives in the forest that no explorer had ever seen. The unknown animal's name is Bigfoot; it has really big feet and really big hands and lives with the animals in the forest, down the hill by the small river. Billy thought it was the most wonderful bedtime story he had ever heard.

Billy knew that his experience was special. Although, he was looking for the very rare white fox, he found something even more special: Billy found Bigfoot. Sometimes one of the rarest animals can be right in front of you. Being patient and kind can help you see everything in the forest.